The River Is My Life

Jocelyn Sigue
Photography by Kim Hairston

Rigby

a division of Reed Elsevier Inc.
500 Coventry Lane
Crystal Lake, IL 60014

00 99
10 9 8 7 6 5 4 3

Printed in Singapore

ISBN 0-7635-3180-4

Interviews can be exciting. One person asks questions, and another person answers them. We read interviews in news stories. Sometimes we see them on television. News reporters ask the questions. Interesting people answer them.

Jocelyn Sigue, news reporter

This is an interview with a man who works on the river, catching oysters. His name is George Ambrose Chisley. His family and friends call him Bo. He will let us call him Bo, too.

Reporter: *What are oysters, Bo? Where do you catch them?*

Bo Chisley: Many people like to eat oysters. These sea animals live in shells that are rough and unevenly shaped. You can find them at the bottom of oceans and rivers. I catch them in the Wicomico River. The river flows for miles near my home, a town called Newburg, Maryland. Newburg is on the eastern shore of the United States. I have lived there my whole life and have been catching oysters for 47 years.

UNITED STATES
Newburg, Maryland
Atlantic Ocean
SCALE
1 inch = 1070 miles
(1722 kilometers)
Newburg, Maryland
Wicomico River

SAL Y

Reporter: *Wow! You've been catching oysters since you were a boy. How did you learn?*

Bo: My family taught me. I have seven brothers and six sisters. We all grew up on the river. My father took his boat out every day to catch oysters. I wanted to be just like him. My older brother Jimmy had a small boat that he let me borrow every day after school. I'd catch the oysters, and Jimmy would sell them to his friends.

Reporter: *When do you catch oysters now?*

Bo: I spend the whole day catching oysters. I start when the sun rises. My partner Chris and I are on my boat at seven o'clock. Chris is like a son to me. I have five sons of my own and one daughter. Sometimes they help us catch oysters, but usually it's just the two of us. It's fun to have someone on the boat with me. We catch oysters in the fall and winter. We let the rest grow during the spring and summer so that we can come back for them later.

Reporter: *Are oysters hard to catch?*

Bo: Yes, sometimes catching them is so hard that Chris and I just want to give up. The oysters are buried beneath the sand at the bottom of the river. We use special tools called tongs to grab them. The tongs are very long because the water is deep. My biggest tongs are 26 feet long. That's about as long as two cars parked end to end. The tongs are made of wood and metal and work like scissors. We slip them into the water and open them when they reach the bottom. Then we close them around a bunch of oysters and pull them up. That's hard work because the tongs are very heavy.

Reporter: *Then what do you do with the oysters?*

Bo: We use a tool to measure the oysters. If they are smaller than three inches long, we have to throw them back. That's because there are laws for oyster catching in the United States. The laws say that the smaller oysters have to stay in the river. By throwing the smaller ones back, we know there will be oysters in the river next year. We catch the most oysters in September. The most we have caught in one day is 9000. By March many oysters have already been caught, and we catch only around 4000 a day. We wish we could catch more.

Reporter: *That still sounds like a lot of oysters. What do you do with the ones you don't throw back?*

Bo: I sell them. Chris and I bring the boat back to the dock at four o'clock every day. We sell our oysters to a man named Butch. He buys the oysters by the bushel. Each bushel holds about 300 oysters. We are paid $18 for every bushel we sell. Chris and I split the money we earn evenly. Butch brings the oysters to another group of people.

Reporter: *What do they do with the oysters?*

Bo: They pull the oysters out of the shells. That's called shucking. You see, you can't eat the shell. It's too hard. You can only eat the meat inside. After they are shucked, the oysters are sold to restaurants and to people who put them in jars for grocery stores. Some may end up on your plate. They can be fried or put in a soup. When they're very fresh, you don't have to cook them at all. I like them raw. That way they keep all of their nutrients. Oysters are really good for you.

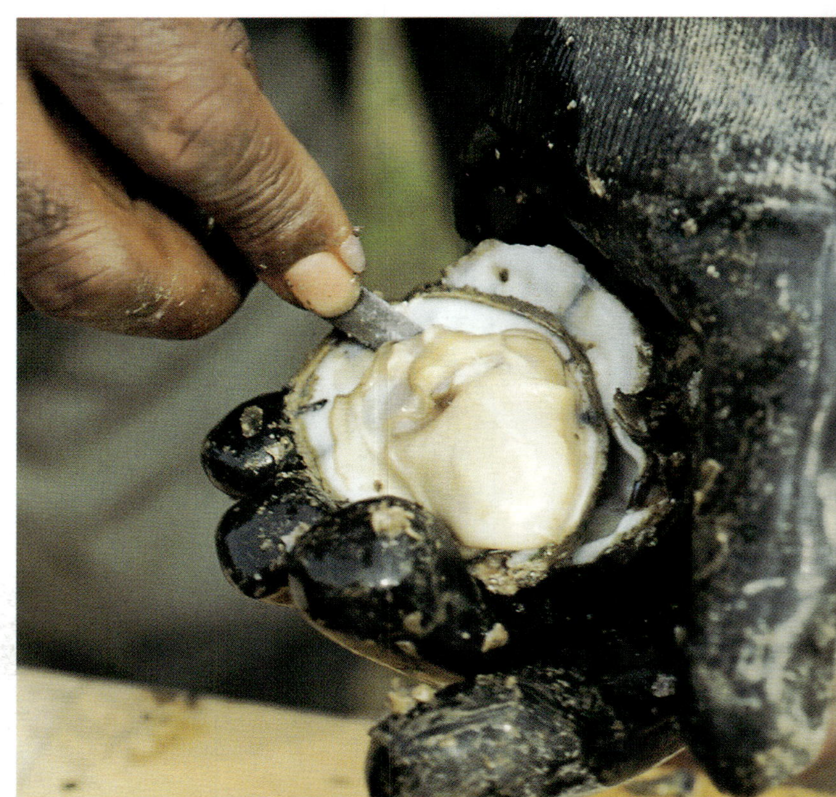

Reporter: *Raw oysters don't look very tasty. Do you ever eat them cooked?*

Bo: Of course! I have eaten oysters since I was a boy. I don't eat them raw all the time. Sometimes Chris and I make oyster soup for lunch. We cook the soup right on the boat. Once in a while, I bring oysters home to my wife. I sit down at the kitchen table, and she cooks them for me. Sometimes I help her cook them. We shuck them, coat them with breading, and fry them. They taste great! There's nothing like the taste of oysters. I don't think there's anything I love to eat more.

Reporter: *What do you like best about your job?*

Bo: There's no place I love more than the river. I've tried other jobs, but I keep coming back to oyster catching. The river is a great place to be. It's peaceful and quiet. Every night when I go to sleep, I know that the next day will be exciting. I will spend it on the river, catching oysters. The river is my life.